Collins
My First Book of
World Flags

D0419653

Collins My First Book of World Flags
Collins
An imprint of HarperCollins Publishers
Westerhill Road
Bishopbriggs
Glasgow G64 2QT

© HarperCollins Publishers 2013
Maps © Collins Bartholomew Ltd 2011

First published 2011
Reprinted 2012
Second edition 2013

ISBN 978-0-00-752125-8

Imp 001

Collins ® is a registered trademark of HarperCollins
Publishers Ltd

All rights reserved. No part of this publication may
be reproduced, stored in a retrieval system, or
transmitted in any form or by any means, electronic,
mechanical, photocopying, recording or otherwise,
without the prior written permission of the publisher
or copyright owners.

The contents of this edition of Collins My First Book
of World Flags are believed correct at the time of
printing. Nevertheless the publishers can accept
no responsibility for errors or omissions, changes
in the detail given, or for any expense or loss
thereby caused.

British Library Cataloguing in Publication Data
A catalogue record for this book is available from the
British Library.

Printed and bound by Imago in Singapore

All mapping in this atlas is generated from Collins
Bartholomew digital databases.
Collins Bartholomew, the UK's leading independent
geographical information supplier, can provide a
digital, custom, and premium mapping service to a
variety of markets.
For further information:
Tel: +44 (0) 141 306 3752
e-mail: collinsbartholomew@harpercollins.co.uk

Visit our websites at:
www.harpercollins.co.uk
www.collinsbartholomew.com
www.collinsmaps.com

Contents

World Flags

Flags are usually associated with countries, nations and international organizations. Flags are everywhere.

They are used in football, racing, industry, schools, by explorers and armies. Flags come in all shapes, sizes and colours.

Europe

Africa

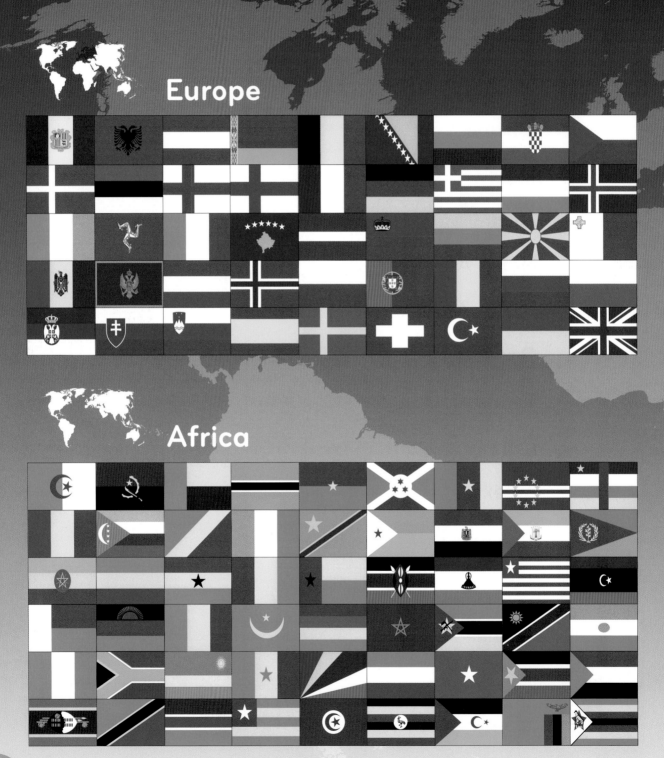

Asia

North America

South America

Oceania

Europe

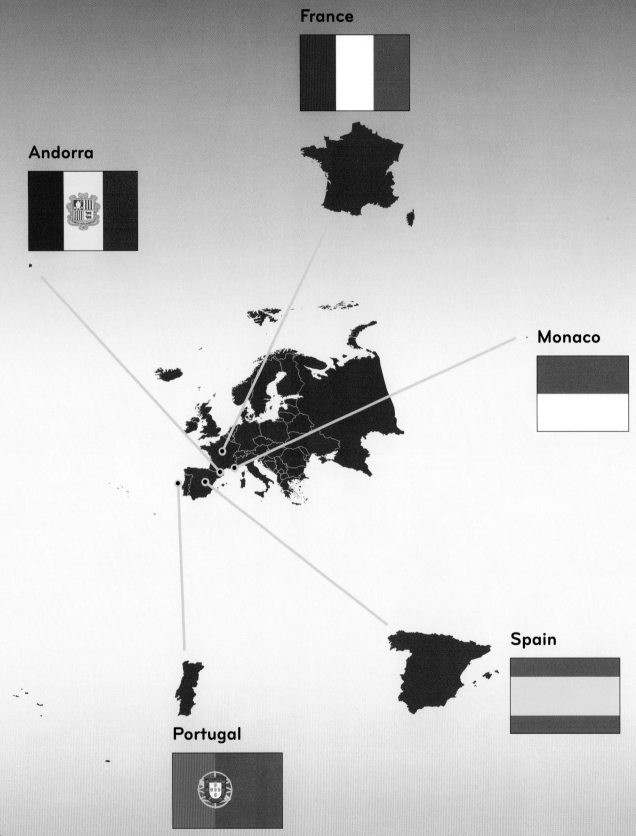

France

Andorra

Monaco

Spain

Portugal

Bullfight
Madrid, Spain

Capital cities

Andorra	Andorra la Vella
France	Paris
Monaco	Monaco-Ville
Portugal	Lisbon
Spain	Madrid

Europe

Iceland

Faroe Islands (Denmark)

Isle of Man (UK)

United Kingdom

Ireland

Jersey (UK)

Guernsey (UK)

Capital cities

Faroe Islands (Denmark)	Tórshavn
Guernsey (UK)	St Peter Port
Iceland	Reykjavík
Ireland	Dublin
Isle of Man (UK)	Douglas
Jersey (UK)	St Helier
United Kingdom	London

Geyser eruption, Iceland

Europe

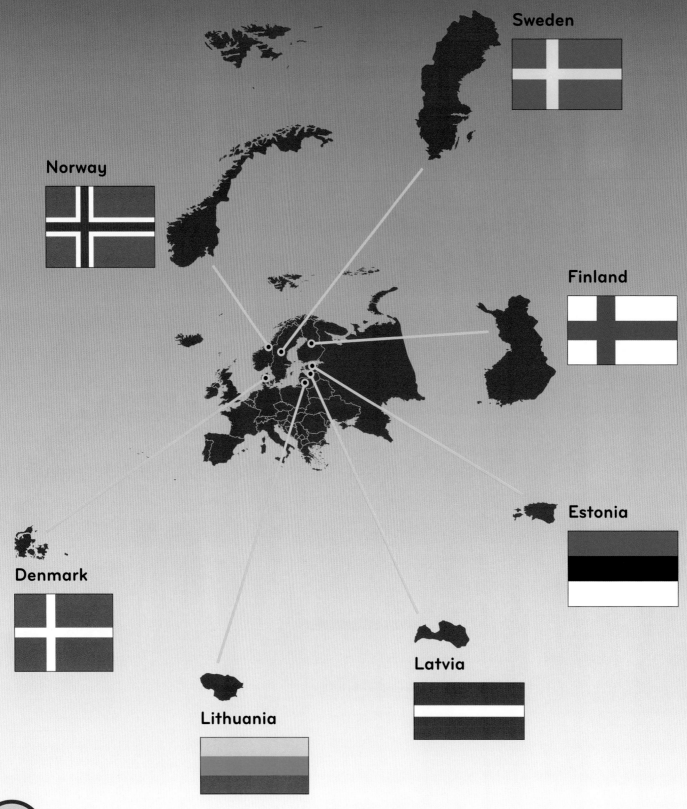

Sweden

Norway

Finland

Denmark

Estonia

Latvia

Lithuania

Capital cities

Denmark	Copenhagen
Estonia	Tallinn
Finland	Helsinki
Latvia	Rīga
Lithuania	Vilnius
Norway	Oslo
Sweden	Stockholm

Reindeer, Sweden

Europe

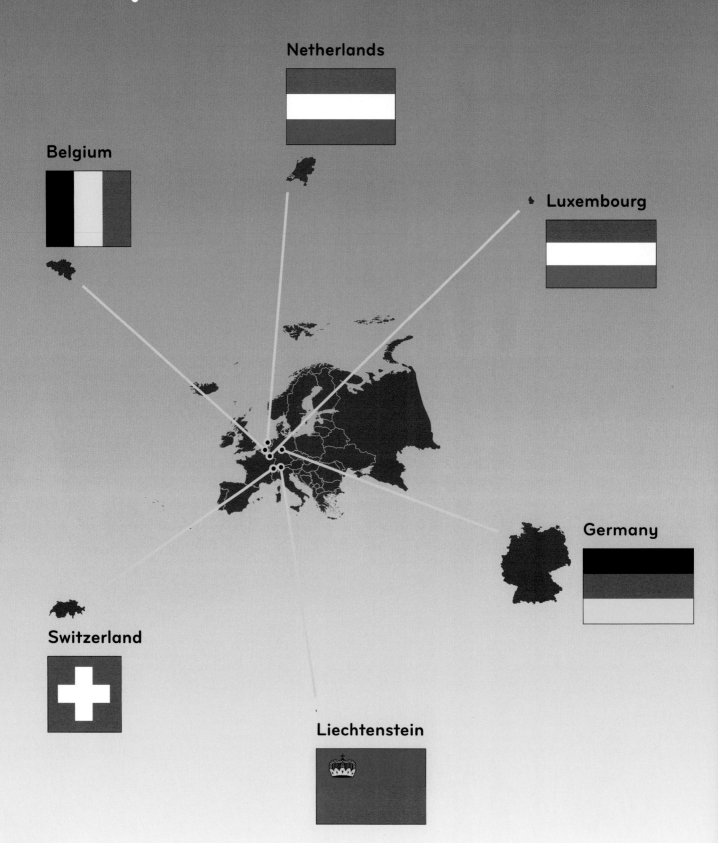

Netherlands

Belgium

Luxembourg

Germany

Switzerland

Liechtenstein

Capital cities

Belgium	Brussels
Germany	Berlin
Liechtenstein	Vaduz
Luxembourg	Luxembourg
Netherlands	Amsterdam / The Hague
Switzerland	Bern

The river Rhine in Koblenz, Germany

Europe

Poland

Czech Republic

Slovakia

Hungary

Austria

Slovenia

Capital cities

Austria	**Vienna**
Czech Republic	**Prague**
Hungary	**Budapest**
Poland	**Warsaw**
Slovakia	**Bratislava**
Slovenia	**Ljubljana**

Church of Our Lady,
Prague, Czech Republic

Europe

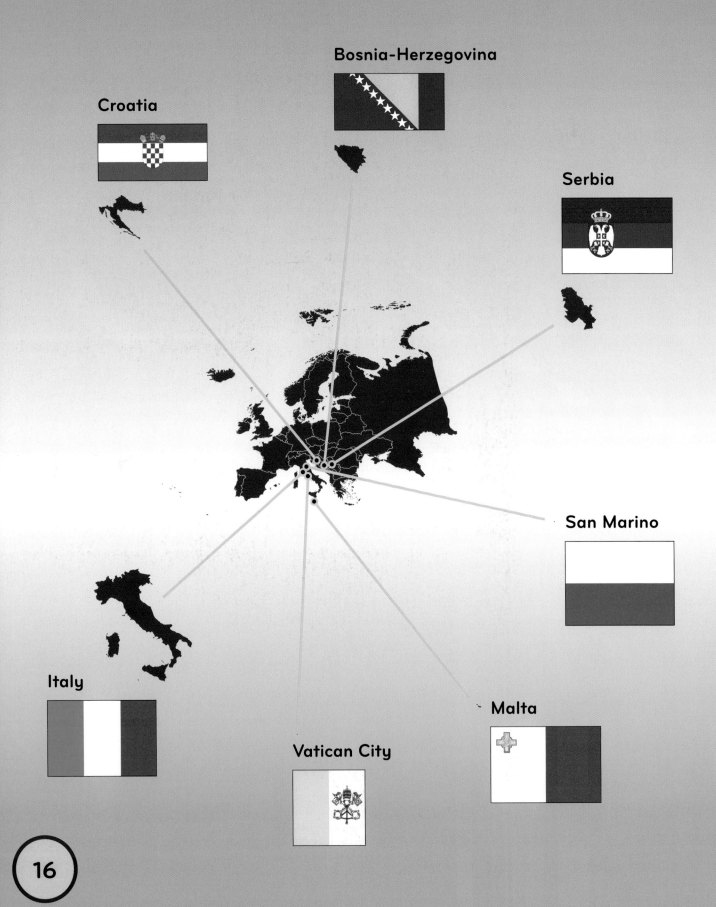

Croatia

Bosnia-Herzegovina

Serbia

San Marino

Italy

Vatican City

Malta

Capital cities

Bosnia-Herzegovina	**Sarajevo**
Croatia	**Zagreb**
Italy	**Rome**
Malta	**Valletta**
San Marino	**San Marino**
Serbia	**Belgrade**
Vatican City	**Vatican City**

Florence, Italy

Europe

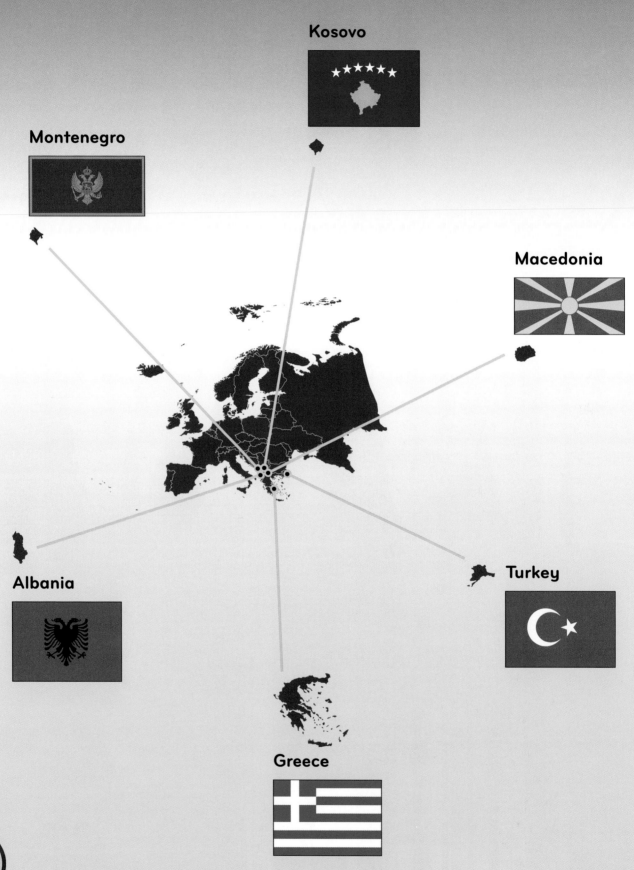

Kosovo

Montenegro

Macedonia

Albania

Turkey

Greece

Capital cities

Albania	**Tirana**
Greece	**Athens**
Kosovo	**Pristina**
Macedonia	**Skopje**
Montenegro	**Podgorica**
Turkey	**Ankara**

Fishing boats in harbour, Greece

Europe

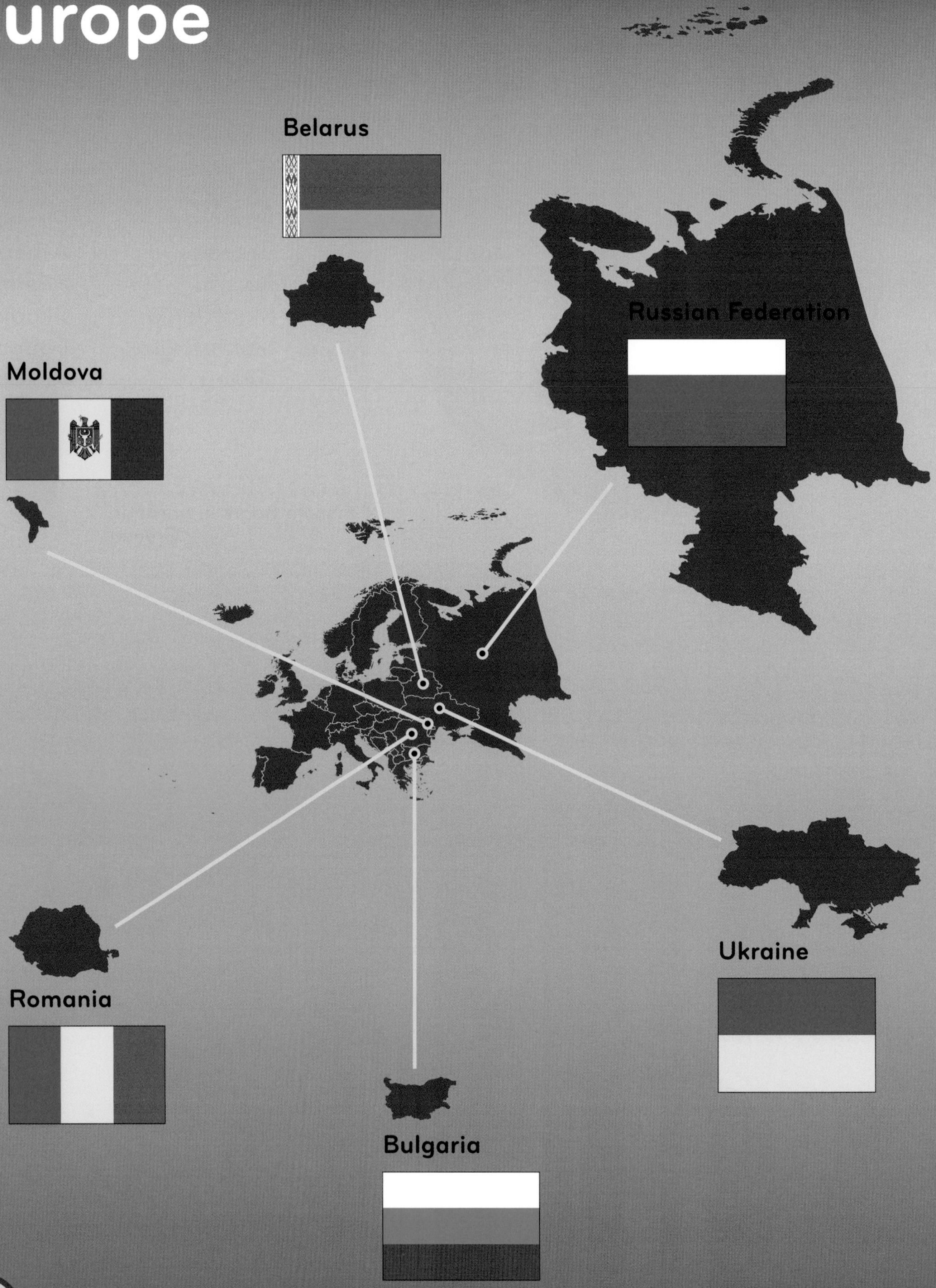

Belarus

Russian Federation

Moldova

Ukraine

Romania

Bulgaria

Capital cities

Belarus	Minsk
Bulgaria	Sofia
Moldova	Chișinău
Romania	Bucharest
Russian Federation	Moscow
Ukraine	Kiev

Cathedral in St Petersburg,
Russian Federation

Africa

Moroccan spices,
Marrakech, Morocco

Capital cities

Algeria	**Algiers**
Cape Verde	**Praia**
Egypt	**Cairo**
Libya	**Tripoli**
Mauritania	**Nouakchott**
Morocco	**Rabat**
Tunisia	**Tunis**
Western Sahara	**Laayoune**

Morocco

Western Sahara

Tunisia

Egypt

Cape Verde

Mauritania

Libya

Algeria

Africa

Traditional African boats, Senegal

Capital cities

Côte d'Ivoire (Ivory Coast)	Yamoussoukro
Guinea	Conakry
Guinea-Bissau	Bissau
Liberia	Monrovia
Mali	Bamako
Senegal	Dakar
Sierra Leone	Freetown
The Gambia	Banjul

Senegal

Mali

The Gambia

Guinea-Bissau

Guinea

Côte d'Ivoire
(Ivory Coast)

Liberia

Sierra Leone

Africa

Capital cities

Benin	Porto-Novo
Burkina Faso	Ouagadougou
Chad	Ndjamena
Ghana	Accra
Niger	Niamey
Nigeria	Abuja
Togo	Lomé

Old rusted cannon in Elmina Castle, Ghana

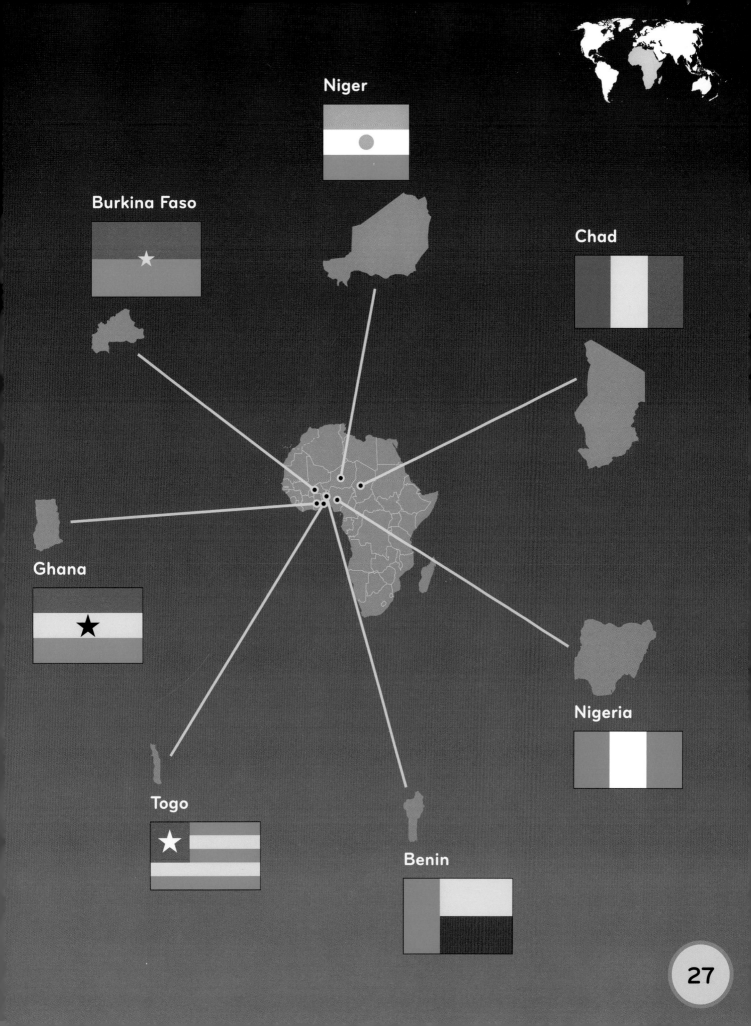

Niger

Burkina Faso

Chad

Ghana

Nigeria

Togo

Benin

27

Africa

Capital cities

Djibouti	Djibouti
Eritrea	Asmara
Ethiopia	Addis Ababa
Kenya	Nairobi
Somalia	Mogadishu
South Sudan	Juba
Sudan	Khartoum
Uganda	Kampala

Hot-air balloon over the Masai Mara, Kenya

Sudan

Eritrea

Djibouti

South Sudan

Somalia

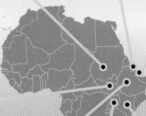

Ethiopia

Kenya

Uganda

Africa

African women praying,
Cameroon

Capital cities

Cameroon	Yaoundé
Central African Republic	Bangui
Equatorial Guinea	Malabo
Gabon	Libreville
St Helena, Ascension and Tristan da Cunha (UK)	Jamestown
São Tomé and Príncipe	São Tomé

Cameroon

Central African Republic

Equatorial Guinea

Gabon

St Helena, Ascension and Tristan da Cunha (UK)

São Tomé and Príncipe

Africa

Silverback gorilla,
Democratic Republic of the Congo

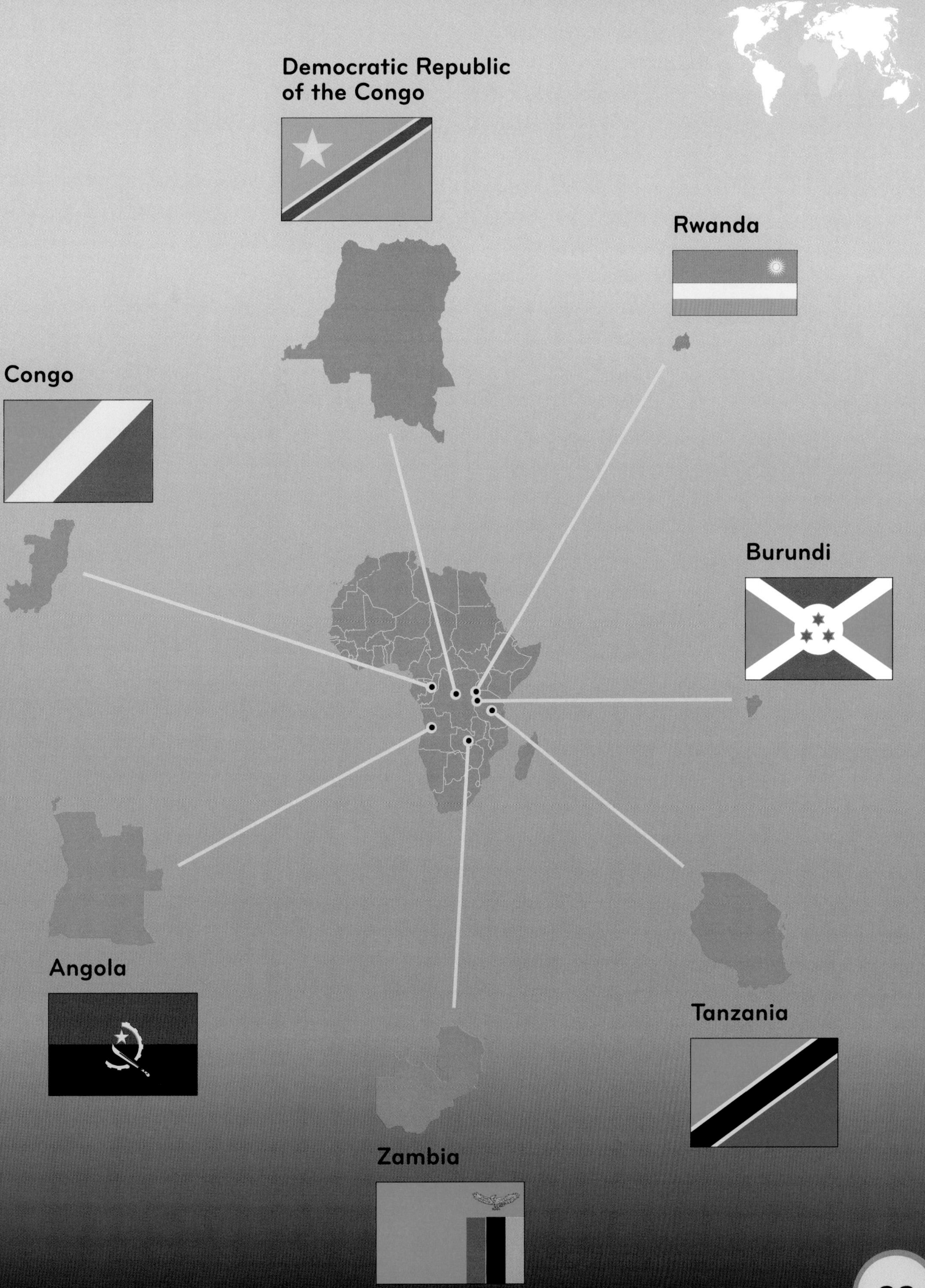

Democratic Republic
of the Congo

Rwanda

Congo

Burundi

Angola

Tanzania

Zambia

Africa

Capital cities

Botswana	Gaborone
Malawi	Lilongwe
Mozambique	Maputo
Namibia	Windhoek
Swaziland	Mbabane
Zimbabwe	Harare

Lioness with young lion cubs,
Kalahari Desert, Botswana

Malawi

Zimbabwe

Mozambique

Namibia

Swaziland

Botswana

Africa

Capital cities

Comoros	**Moroni**
Lesotho	**Maseru**
Madagascar	**Antananarivo**
Mauritius	**Port Louis**
Mayotte (France)	**Dzaoudzi**
Réunion (France)	**St-Denis**
Seychelles	**Victoria**
South Africa	**Pretoria / Cape Town / Bloemfontein**

Springbok,
South Africa

Mayotte (France)

Seychelles

Comoros

Madagascar

South Africa

Mauritius

Lesotho

Réunion (France)

Asia

Uzbekistan

Georgia

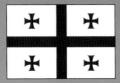

Armenia

Azerbaijan

Turkmenistan

Capital cities

Armenia	Yerevan
Azerbaijan	Baku
Georgia	T'bilisi
Turkmenistan	Ashgabat
Uzbekistan	Tashkent

Offshore rigs in the Caspian Sea,
Baku, Azerbaijan

Asia

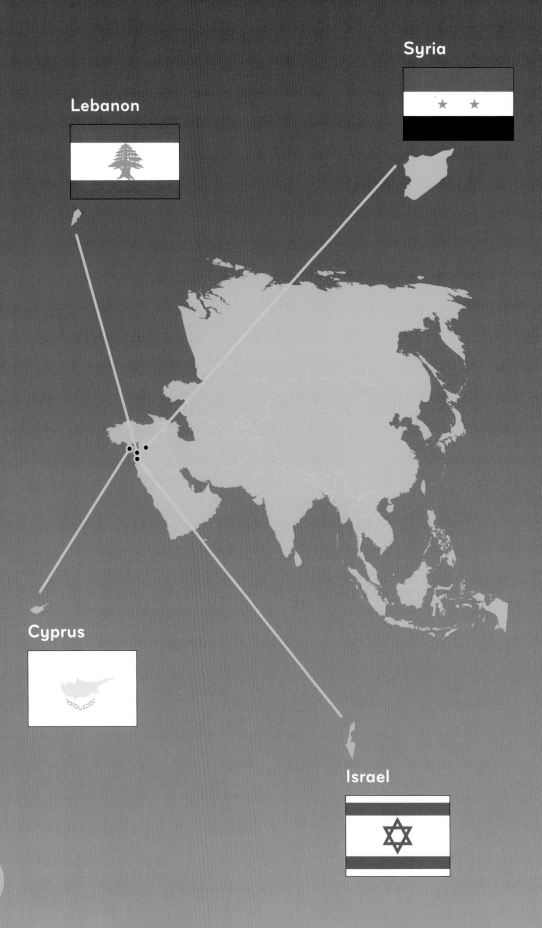

Lebanon

Syria

Cyprus

Israel

The Temple Mount,
Jerusalem, Israel

Capital cities

Cyprus	**Nicosia**
Israel	**Jerusalem***
Lebanon	**Beirut**
Syria	**Damascus**

*not internationally recognised

Asia

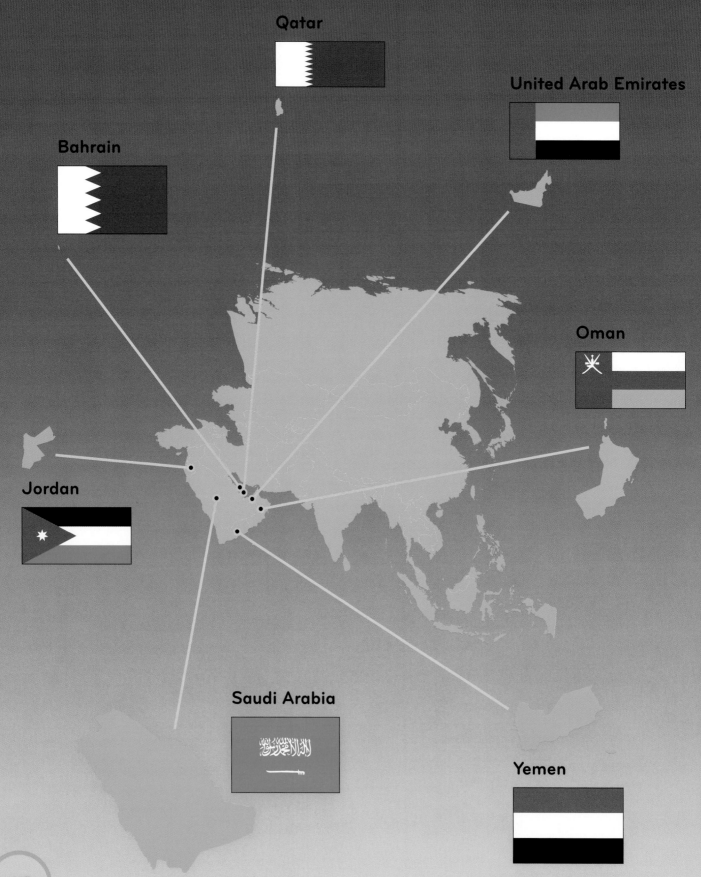

Qatar

United Arab Emirates

Bahrain

Oman

Jordan

Saudi Arabia

Yemen

Capital cities

Bahrain	Manama
Jordan	Amman
Oman	Muscat
Qatar	Doha
Saudi Arabia	Riyadh
United Arab Emirates	Abu Dhabi
Yemen	San'a

Camels in the desert,
Saudi Arabia

Asia

Iran

Iraq

Afghanistan

Kuwait

Bangladesh

Pakistan

India

Capital cities

Afghanistan	Kabul
Bangladesh	Dhaka
India	New Delhi
Iran	Tehran
Iraq	Baghdad
Kuwait	Kuwait
Pakistan	Islamabad

Taj Mahal, India

Asia

Mongolia

China

Bhutan

Nepal

Kazakhstan

Tajikistan

Kyrgyzstan

Capital cities

Bhutan	**Thimphu**
China	**Beijing**
Kazakhstan	**Astana**
Kyrgyzstan	**Bishkek**
Mongolia	**Ulan Bator**
Nepal	**Kathmandu**
Tajikistan	**Dushanbe**

Giant panda, China

Asia

Laos

Vietnam

Myanmar (Burma)

Cambodia

Thailand

Malaysia

Singapore

Capital cities

Cambodia	Phnom Penh
Laos	Vientiane
Malaysia	Kuala Lumpur / Putrajaya
Myanmar (Burma)	Nay Pyi Taw
Singapore	Singapore
Thailand	Bangkok
Vietnam	Hanoi

Orang-utan and her baby,
Borneo, Malaysia

Asia

North Korea

Japan

South Korea

Philippines

Palau

Capital cities

Japan	**Tokyo**
North Korea	**Pyongyang**
Palau	**Melekeok**
Philippines	**Manila**
South Korea	**Seoul**

Tarsier, Philippines

Asia

Sri Lanka

Maldives

Brunei

Indonesia

East Timor

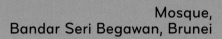

Mosque,
Bandar Seri Begawan, Brunei

Capital cities

Brunei	**Bandar Seri Begawan**
East Timor	**Dili**
Indonesia	**Jakarta**
Maldives	**Male**
Sri Lanka	**Sri Jayewardenepura Kotte**

North America

Grand Canyon, Arizona,
United States of America

Capital cities

Bermuda (UK)	Hamilton
Canada	Ottawa
Greenland (Denmark)	Nuuk
St Pierre and Miquelon (France)	St-Pierre
United States of America	Washington D.C.

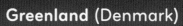

Canada

Greenland (Denmark)

St Pierre and Miquelon (France)

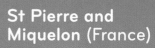

Bermuda (UK)

United States of America

North America

Caribbean cruise ship,
Curaçao

Capital cities

Aruba (Netherlands)	Oranjestad
Cayman Islands (UK)	George Town
Cuba	Havana
Curaçao (Netherlands)	Willemstad
Dominican Republic	Santo Domingo
Haiti	Port-au-Prince
Jamaica	Kingston
Puerto Rico (USA)	San Juan
The Bahamas	Nassau
Turks and Caicos Islands (UK)	Grand Turk

Cuba

The Bahamas

Turks and Caicos Islands (UK)

Cayman Islands (UK)

Puerto Rico (USA)

Jamaica

Haiti

Dominican Republic

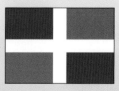

Aruba (Netherlands)

Curaçao (Netherlands)

North America

Capital cities

Anguilla (UK)	The Valley
Antigua and Barbuda	St John's
Barbados	Bridgetown
Dominica	Roseau
Grenada	St George's
Guadeloupe (France)	Basse-Terre
Martinique (France)	Fort-de-France
Montserrat (UK)	Brades
St Kitts and Nevis	Basseterre
St Lucia	Castries
St Vincent and the Grenadines	Kingstown
Trinidad and Tobago	Port of Spain
Virgin Islands (UK)	Road Town
Virgin Islands (USA)	Charlotte Amalie

Anguilla (UK)

Antigua and Barbuda

Guadeloupe (France)

Virgin Islands (UK)

Dominica

Virgin Islands (USA)

Martinique (France)

St Kitts and Nevis

St Lucia

Montserrat (UK)

Barbados

Grenada

Trinidad and Tobago

St Vincent and the Grenadines

North America

Capital cities

Belize	Belmopan
Costa Rica	San José
El Salvador	San Salvador
Guatemala	Guatemala City
Honduras	Tegucigalpa
Mexico	Mexico City
Nicaragua	Managua
Panama	Panama City

Toucan, Costa Rica

60

Mexico

Belize

Honduras

Guatemala

Nicaragua

El Salvador

Panama

Costa Rica

South America

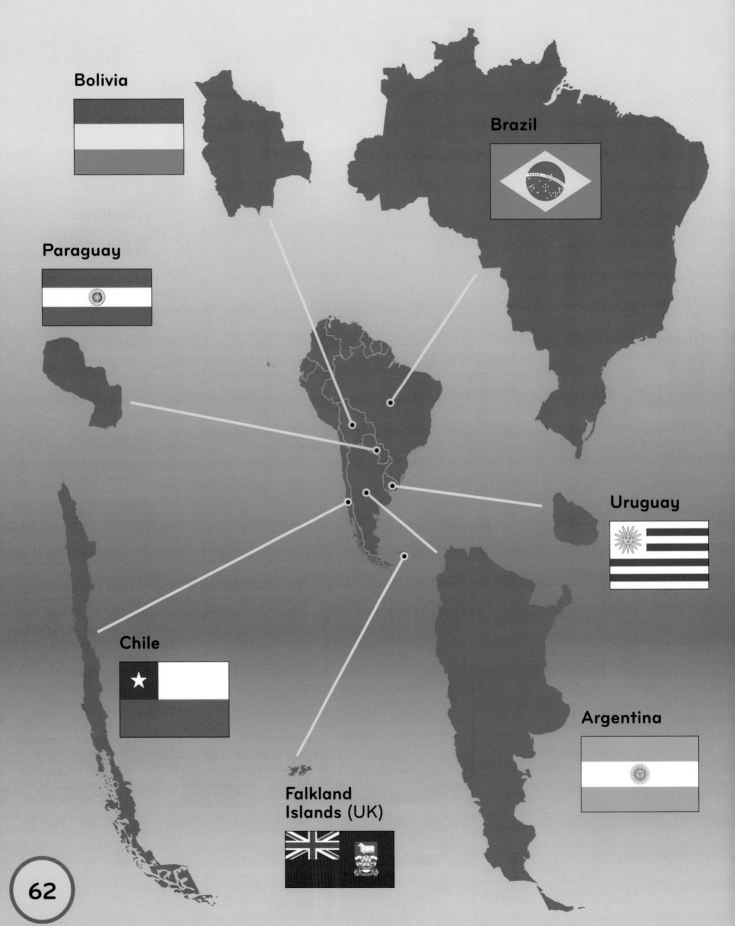

Bolivia

Paraguay

Brazil

Uruguay

Chile

Argentina

Falkland
Islands (UK)

62

Capital cities

Argentina	Buenos Aires
Bolivia	La Paz / Sucre
Brazil	Brasília
Chile	Santiago
Falkland Islands (UK)	Stanley
Paraguay	Asunción
Uruguay	Montevideo

Glacier in Patagonia, Argentina

South America

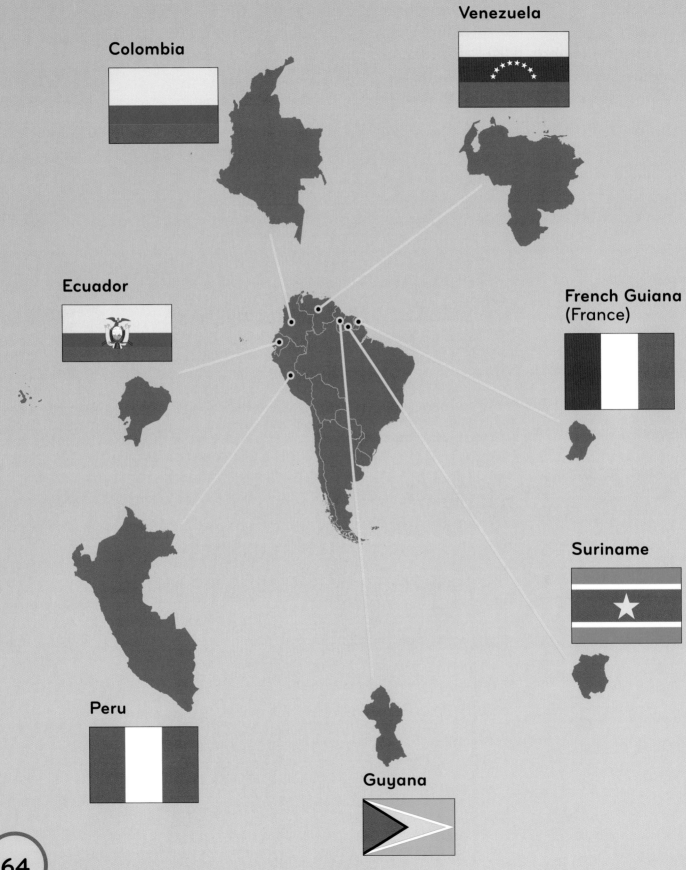

Colombia

Venezuela

Ecuador

French Guiana
(France)

Peru

Suriname

Guyana

Capital cities

Colombia	**Bogotá**
Ecuador	**Quito**
French Guiana (France)	**Cayenne**
Guyana	**Georgetown**
Peru	**Lima**
Suriname	**Paramaribo**
Venezuela	**Caracas**

Machu Picchu, Peru

Oceania

Capital cities

Australia	Canberra
New Zealand	Wellington
Papua New Guinea	Port Moresby

Sydney Opera House,
Sydney, Australia

Papua New Guinea

Australia

New Zealand

Oceania

Capital cities

Federated States of Micronesia
Palikir
Marshall Islands   Delap-Uliga-Djarrit
Nauru   Yaren
Solomon Islands   Honiara

Rainbow lorikeets,
Solomon Islands

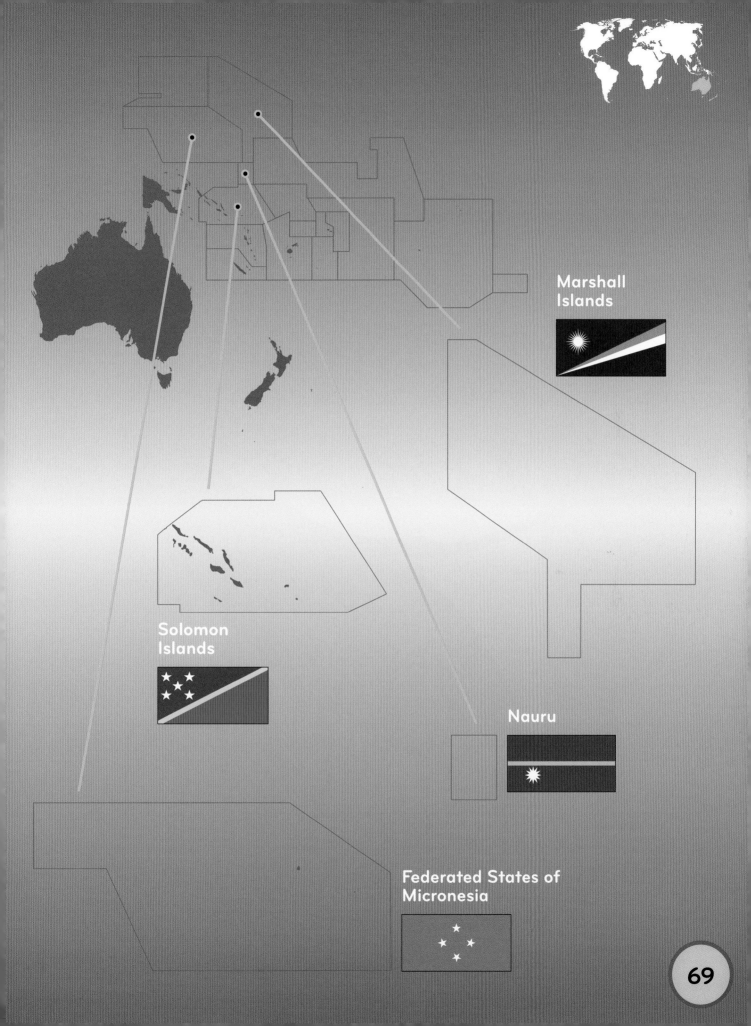

Marshall
Islands

Solomon
Islands

Nauru

Federated States of
Micronesia

Oceania

Capital cities

Fiji	Suva
New Caledonia (France)	Nouméa
Tuvalu	Vaiaku
Vanuatu	Port Vila

Fishing, Fiji

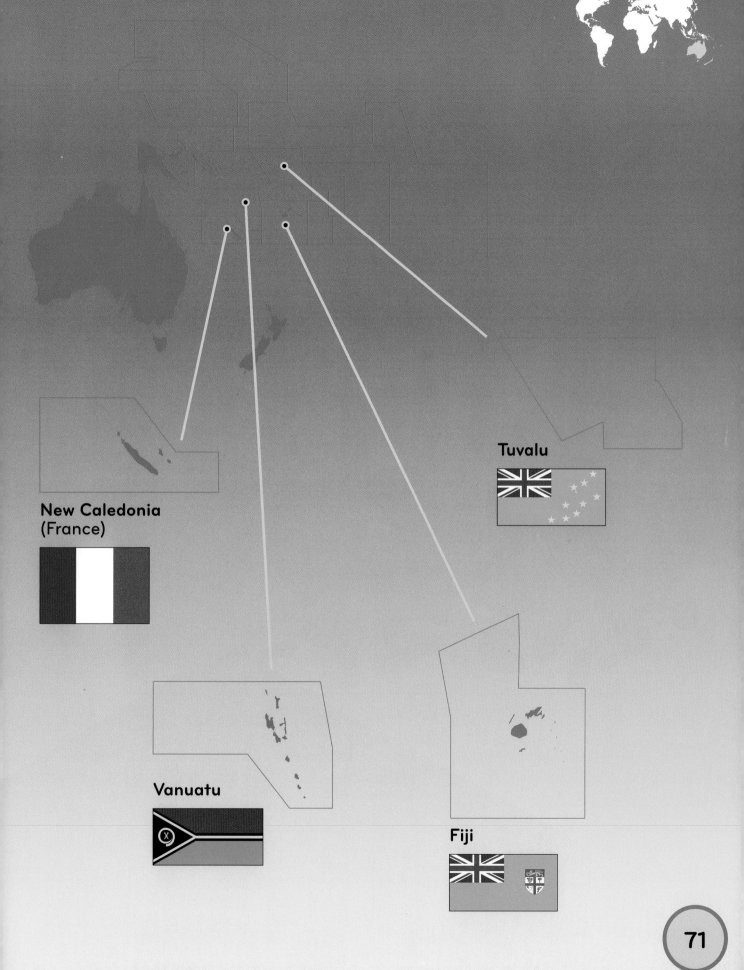

New Caledonia
(France)

Tuvalu

Vanuatu

Fiji

Oceania

Shell fans, Cook Islands

**Cook Islands
(New Zealand)**

Samoa

Tonga

**American
Samoa (USA)**

Kiribati

Types of Flags

Flags with animals

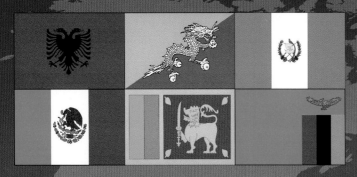

Flags featuring a star or stars

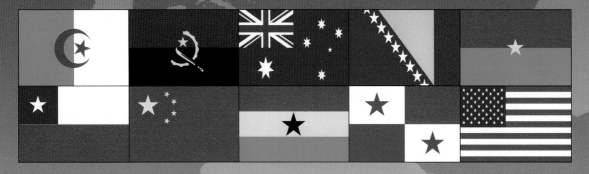

Flags featuring a sun

Flags with a moon

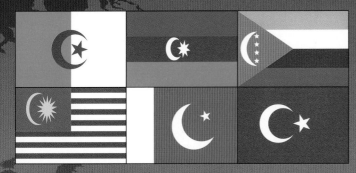

Flags with triangles

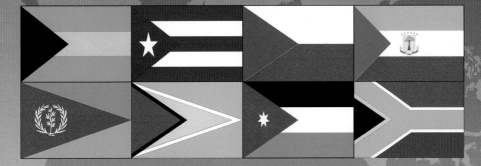

Striped flags

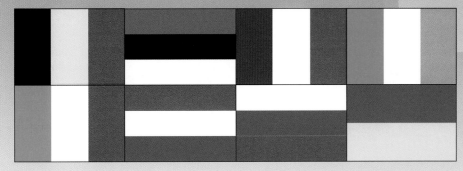

Quiz

Whose flag is this?

There are 20 country flags and 20 country names shown below.
Match up the country names to their flag.

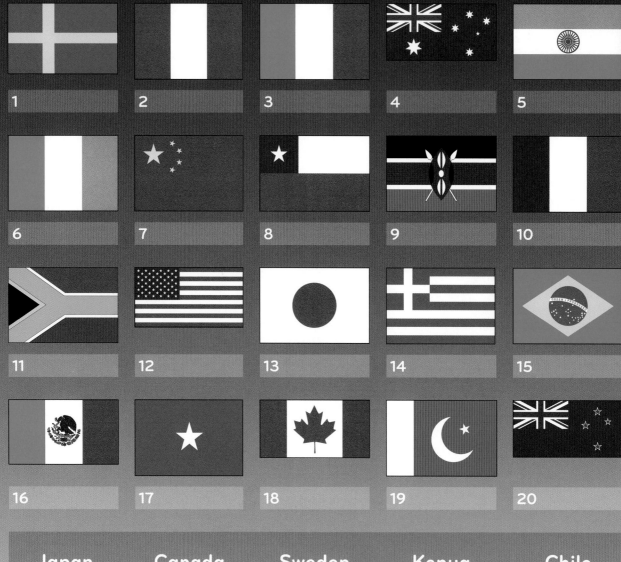

Japan	Canada	Sweden	Kenya	Chile
Greece	Australia	USA	South Africa	Brazil
Somalia	Pakistan	France	Ireland	Peru
India	New Zealand	China	Mexico	Italy

Spot the difference!

Look at the pairs of flags below. Guess the country each belongs to and find the difference between each pair.

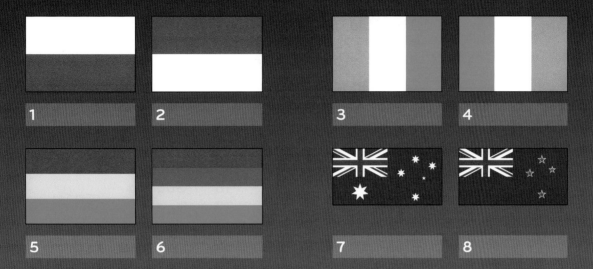

Match the country to its flag

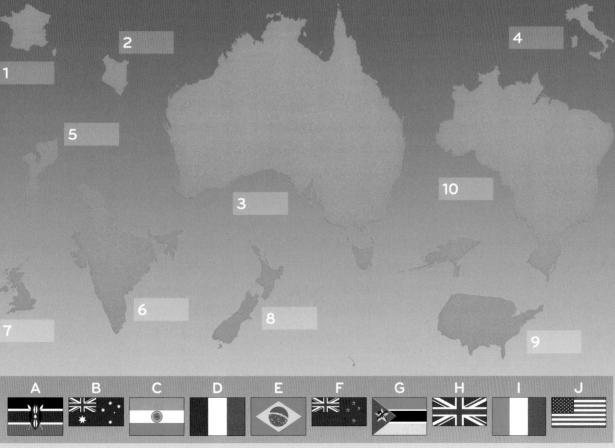

Answers at the back of the book

Index

Lithuania	10	Peru	64	Tajikistan	46
Luxembourg	12	Philippines	50	Tanzania	33
Macedonia	18	Poland	14	Thailand	48
Madagascar	37	Portugal	6	Togo	27
Malawi	35	Puerto Rico (USA)	57	Tonga	73
Malaysia	48	Qatar	42	Trinidad and Tobago	59
Maldives	52	Réunion (France)	37	Tristan da Cunha (UK)	31
Mali	25	Romania	20	Tunisia	23
Malta	16	Russian Federation	20	Turkey	18
Marshall Islands	69	Rwanda	33	Turkmenistan	38
Martinique (France)	59	St Helena (UK)	31	Turks and Caicos Islands	
Mauritania	23	St Kitts and Nevis	59	(UK)	57
Mauritius	37	St Lucia	59	Tuvalu	71
Mayotte (France)	37	St Pierre and Miquelon		Uganda	29
Mexico	61	(France)	55	Ukraine	20
Moldova	20	St Vincent and the		United Arab Emirates	42
Monaco	6	Grenadines	59	United Kingdom	8
Mongolia	46	Samoa	73	United States of	
Montenegro	18	San Marino	16	America	55
Montserrat (UK)	59	São Tomé and Príncipe	31	Uruguay	62
Morocco	23	Saudi Arabia	42	Uzbekistan	38
Mozambique	35	Senegal	25	Vanuatu	71
Myanmar (Burma)	48	Serbia	16	Vatican City	16
Namibia	35	Seychelles	37	Venezuela	64
Nauru	69	Sierra Leone	25	Vietnam	48
Nepal	46	Singapore	48	Virgin Islands (UK)	59
Netherlands	12	Slovakia	14	Virgin Islands (USA)	59
New Caledonia		Slovenia	14	Western Sahara	23
(France)	71	Solomon Islands	69	Yemen	42
New Zealand	67	Somalia	29	Zambia	33
Nicaragua	61	South Africa	37	Zimbabwe	35
Niger	27	South Korea	50		
Nigeria	27	South Sudan	29		
North Korea	50	Spain	6		
Norway	10	Sri Lanka	52		
Oman	42	Sudan	29		
Pakistan	44	Suriname	64		
Palau	50	Swaziland	35		
Panama	61	Sweden	10		
Papua New Guinea	67	Switzerland	12		
Paraguay	62	Syria	40		

Quiz answers

Quiz 1 (page 76)

Whose flag is this?

1 Sweden	2 Peru	3 Italy	4 Australia	5 India
6 Ireland	7 China	8 Chile	9 Kenya	10 France
11 South Africa	12 USA	13 Japan	14 Greece	15 Brazil
16 Mexico	17 Somalia	18 Canada	19 Pakistan	20 New Zealand

Quiz 2 (page 77)

Spot the difference!
1. Poland flag has red stripe at the bottom of the flag 2. Indonesia has red stripe at the top.
3. Cote d'Ivoire and 4. Ireland have stripes in a different order.
5. Bolivia and 6. Mauritius have a different number of stripes.
7. Australia flag has white stars 8. New Zealand has red stars.

Quiz 3 (page 77)

Match the country to its flag

1 France D		2 Kenya A	
3 Australia B		4 Italy I	
5 Mozambique G		6 India C	
7 UK H		8 New Zealand F	
9 USA J		10 Brazil E	

Image credits

Images from Shutterstock.com

Cover image and Title image ©esfera, p7 Bullfighter ©Fernando Cortes, p7 paris ©sabri deniz kizil, p9 Geyser ©Cher_Nika, p9 London © Cihan Demirok, CIDEPIX, p11 Reindeer ©Andreas Gradin, p11 SNOWY ©GoodMood Photo, p13 Koblenz ©Jo Chambers, p13 Windmills ©Kozyrin Ivan, p15 Prague ©Artur Bogacki, p15 Mountains ©Kozoriz Yuriy, p17 Florence ©Baloncici, p17 Italian countryside ©Josch, p19 Greek fishing boats ©Ivonne Wierink, p19 Greek ©grafica, p21 St Petersburg ©Liudmila Gridina, p21 Marsh ©Piko72, p22 Moroccan spices ©Daleen Loest, p22 Pyramids ©Boguslaw Mazur, p24 Boats in Senegal ©Kirsz Marcin, p24 Blue African landscape ©ducu59us, p26 Elmina castle ©Steve Heap, p26 Oil rig ©astudio, p28 Hot Air balloon ©Paul Banton, p28 African hunter ©Redsapphire, p30 African women praying ©POZZO DI BORGO Thomas, p30 Green forest ©Binkski, p32 Gorilla ©Miranda van der Kroft, p32 African landscape ©ksena2you, p34 Lions ©EcoPrint, p34 Sunset on desert ©oriori, p36 Sprinbok ©EcoPrint, p36 ringed tailed lemur ©veselin gajin, p36 kudu ©electra, p39 Oil rig Baku ©Elnur, p39 Mount Elbrus ©Julia Dolzhenko, p41 Temple Mount ©Alexander Ishchenko, p41 moon night ©Wilm Ihlenfeld, p43 Camels in S Arabia ©David Steele, p43 dubai ©ImageTeam, p45 Taj Mahal ©Pborowka, p45 Indian elephants ©isaxar, p47 Panda ©df028, p47 chinese pavillion ©Alexander Smulskiy, p49 Orangutan ©Kjersti Joergensen, p49 Kuala Lumpur ©Inis Vikmanis, p51 Tarsier ©Edwin Veren, p51 Japan ©nadiya_sergey, p53 Mosque in Brunei ©Ralf Siemieniec, p53 Forest ©Binkski, p54 Grand Canyon ©Tom Hirtreiter, p54 Liberty ©nameless, p56 Cruise ship Bahamas ©Chris Jenner, p56 caribbean ©Mushakesa, p58 tropical beach ©untung, p60 Toucan ©Roberts.J, p60 Mexico ©Katsianyna, p63 Patagonia ©javarman, p63 Rio ©Athanasia Nomikou, p65 Machu Picchu ©agap, p65 forest ©Sergey Ok, p66 sydney Harbour ©Taras Vyshnya, p66 Kangaroos ©Stasys Eidiejus, p68 Lorikeet ©Uryadnikov Sergey, p68 frogman ©Steyno&Stitch, p70 Fiji fishing ©YUVIS studio, p70 Whale ©Daniel Wiedemann, p72 Cook Island fans ©gmanz, p72 Volcano ©iraladybird.